Deliverance
Your Key to Freedom

Live the Christian life you have always desired by being set free through deliverance!

BY PASTOR MARIA YIANGOU

Kingdom Publishers

www.kingdompublishers.co.uk

DELIVERANCE – YOUR KEY TO FREEDOM

Copyright © Maria Yiangou 2016

Illustrated cover design by Cecilia Hassan

All rights reserved

No part of this book may be reproduced in any form by photocopyingor any electronic or mechanical means, including information storageor retrieval systems, without permission in writing from both thecopyright owner and the publisher of the book.

The right of Maria Yiangou to be identified as the author of this work hasbeen asserted by him/her in accordance with the Copyright, Designs andPatents Act 1988 and any subsequent amendments thereto.

Unless otherwise indicated, all Scripture quotations are taken from the NewLiving Translation of the Bible.

A catalogue record for this book is available from the British Library

ISBN 978-0-9935959-2-9

2nd Edition by Kingdom Publishers
Published by Kingdom Publishers 2016
Kingdom Publishers, London, England

Preface

As directed by the Holy Spirit to start writing books after five years of being a co-founding pastor of a deliverance ministry and another five years of being in training for ministry, I have taken the step of obedience to follow the calling that God has for my life and to not only preach the undiluted and uncompromising gospel of Jesus Christ of Nazareth but to also start writing books from all the experiences I have had as a Senior Pastor, Preacher, Teacher, Deliverance Minister and being under the discipleship of great men of God. My time has come to write from all that I have seen and experienced and hope you will be blessed by this very practical book.

The reason I felt to write this title – ***Deliverance – Your Key to Freedom!*** – is that I found that many born-again Christians still had problems such as addictions, anger, lust and poverty spirit, but didn't understand how to deal with these problems, not knowing they can be set free from these issues through deliverance.

Hence by writing this book I hope it will answer many of your questions and be a great blessing to you. But before we begin, I would like you to repeat this prayer:

Maria Yiangou

Lord Jesus, thank you for all your goodness and mercy upon my life

Thank you for saving me through undeserved favour, your wonderful grace

Thank you that I have come to know you

Thank you for your love and goodness over my home, family, children and life

I commit reading this book into your hands and I pray that you will help me understand all that I read, that it will make sense to me and it will answer all my questions on what it means to be set free in Jesus' Name!

Prayer of Salvation

If you have not received Jesus Christ as your Personal Saviour, recite this prayer:

Lord Jesus, as it says in your Word, John 3:3, unless we are born again by repenting of our sins, we will not see the Kingdom of Heaven.

I now repent of all my sins, I ask that you forgive me of everything I have done, knowingly and unknowingly and I ask you Jesus to come into my heart as my saviour and save me of my sins in Jesus Name! Amen.

Now it is important to find a good Biblebelieving church that moves in the anointing and power of the Holy Spirit so your life can be transformed and you will become Christ-like in your character, attitude and mind!

Maria Yiangou

I dedicate this book to all Christians who are seeking deliverance and, by the Power of God, are ready to be set free! Thank you for choosing this book to learn more about deliverance and walk in the freedom Jesus died for on the cross of Calvary!

Deliverance – Your Key to Freedom

Contents

Chapter 1
- Why deliverance? ... 12

Chapter 2
- How can I be set free? ... 19

Chapter 3
- How do I maintain my deliverance? ... 28

Chapter 4
- What other ways can demons enter your life? ... 41

Chapter 5
- What types of Spirits are there? ... 45

Chapter 6
- Spirits and their functions explained in ... 53
- more detail ... 53

Chapter 7
- Becoming a Deliverance Minister ... 67

Chapter 8
- My personal experience of deliverance ... 69

Chapter 9
- Test your knowledge on deliverance ... 73

DELIVERANCE – YOUR KEY TO FREEDOM

Deliverance – Your Key to Freedom

Chapter 1
Why deliverance?

Deliverance is a very controversial topic, and that isn't a surprise, due to so many beliefs and ideas about it. One thing is for sure, the Devil hates this subject and will try anything to stop you understanding, reading or moving into deliverance or reading this book or attending a church that operates in deliverance! Know this: Jesus was a DELIVERER and had the most powerful deliverance ministry on the face of the earth! So what is deliverance? It is casting out spirits and even demons from people.

Many of you will even ask: Are there such things as spirits, demons and the Devil? Well, if you believe in the Bible, then you will believe the Devil and demons exist! Read what Jesus says in Luke 10:18: *"I saw Satan falling like lightning."* So, if Jesus says He saw Satan falling like lightning, then this instantly proves there is Satan!

So who is Satan that the Bible refers to more than one hundred times… as Satan, as the devil, as Lucifer? He is a fallen angel, according to Ezekiel 28: 12 – 18:

"You were the model of perfection, full of wisdom and exquisite in beauty. You were in Eden, the garden of God. Your clothing was adorned with every precious stone, red carnelian, pale-green peridot, white moonstone, blue-green beryl, onyx, green jasper, blue lapis lazuli, turquoise, and emerald – all beautifully crafted for you and set in the finest gold. They were given to you on the day you were created. I ordained and anointed you as the mighty angelic guardian. You had access to the holy mountain of God and walked among the stones of fire. You were blameless in all

you did from the day you were created until the day evil was found in you. Your rich commerce led you to violence, and you sinned. So I banished you in disgrace from the mountain of God. I expelled you, O mighty guardian, from your place among the stones of fire. Your heart was filled with pride because of all your beauty. Your wisdom was corrupted by your love of splendour. So I threw you to the ground and exposed you to the curious gaze of kings. You defiled your sanctuaries with your many sins and your dishonest trade. So I brought fire out from within you, and it consumed you. I reduced you to ashes on the ground in the sight of all who were watching."

So from the above verses, Satan was a beautiful angel that was filled with pride due to his beauty. However, he committed many sins and became evil, and hence he was banished from heaven.

Revelation 12: 9 says, *"This great dragon – the ancient serpent called the Devil, or Satan, the one deceiving the whole world – was thrown down to the earth with all his angels."*

The above verse shows us that, when the Devil was thrown out of Heaven, so were angels that rebelled with him. These angels are now known as demons, which are under submission to Satan, and they deceive and influence humans. In Acts 10:38, it actually says that people are under the Devil's power! This shows us that Satan and his demons influence humans into doing evil.

What kind of evil, you may ask? I will give you a few examples as to under what demonic oppression you may be under, such as lust, sexual immorality, deceit, jealousy, depression, addiction, *etc*.

Ephesians 2: 1 – 2 says:

> "Once you were dead because of your disobedience and your many sins. You used to live in sin, just like the rest of the world, obeying the Devil – the commander of the powers in the unseen world. He is the spirit at work in the hearts of those who refuse to obey God."

You may argue with me, saying that you never obeyed the Devil; well, living in sin, the Bible says you did… and you probably didn't realise you were doing so… you were allowing your flesh to follow its sinful nature. However, now that you are born again and have accepted Christ as your Personal Saviour, that needs to change… but there is a tug between good and evil. You may be trying not to fall into temptation and sin but cannot help yourself, and every time, you fall into the same sinful desire that you know the Bible says not to. You are not the only one! Millions of Christians around the world have the same problem, and it is only through the power and the blood of Jesus Christ of Nazareth and through his delivering anointing that you can be set free. Once he sets you free and you continue living right, then you will be free indeed! Awesome! So every spirit that has oppressed you and came upon you to cause you to sin with deliverance you will be set free from, and live the righteous and holy life Christ intended you to live. Every time Satan and his demons will be knocking at the door trying to inhabit you, you will have the ability to say 'no' once you have been set free. And yes, he and his demons can inhabit humans.

A human being has three parts: body, mind (soul) and spirit (1 Thessalonians 5:23). The spirit of a human being belongs to God, and once we have been born again it revives, becomes spiritually born and is united to the Holy Spirit and dwells in the Spirit of Man. However, the body and mind (soul) can be afflicted by evil spirits, and this is where the deliverance ministry is required. Demons afflict people through their mind and physical bodies. For instance, somebody can have sickness in their body; this is usually spiritual, and a demon is afflicting the body. If somebody is having problems mentally, again, this is through a spirit.

Demons or spirits can oppress or possess a person. Oppression is when a spirit is constantly bombarding your mind with thoughts, such as fear, anger, jealousy, sexual perversions, *etc*. Possession is actually when the demon has possessed the person and is controlling them to behave in certain ways. For example, when the person has a demon of anger and rage, they can get out of control, and nothing and no-one can stop them getting angry, which can lead to violence against other people. If a person is oppressed by a spirit consistently, and the spirit is not commanded to leave, then this will most likely
lead to possession.

Let us look at examples in the Bible of people being afflicted by demons:

Luke 4: 33 – 36 says:

> *Once when he was in the synagogue, a man possessed by a demon – an evil spirit – began shouting at Jesus, "Go away! Why are you interfering with us, Jesus of Nazareth? Have you come to destroy us? I know who you are – the Holy One of God!"*

> *Jesus cut him short. "Be quiet! Come out of the man," he ordered. At that, the demon threw the man to the floor as the crowd watched; then it came out of him without hurting him further."*

From reading the above scripture, we learn the following: that a person can be possessed by a demon: the spirit was shouting out, basically speaking through the person, while he was conscious. So demons can talk through people, and I have witnessed this many times when delivering people: that they start talking. Their voice and face change when spirits are speaking through them. However, we must not ask questions or entertain them, as demons do lie. Demons are scared of Jesus, His presence and the anointing, as they are scared that He will destroy them. They know Jesus is the Holy One of God and, hence, they will know His people. Jesus did not entertain demons; He said to them to be quiet and to come out, and immediately the man threw himself on the floor, probably jerking or shouting, as the spirit was coming out.

Matthew 17: 14 – 20 says:

And when they came to the crowd, a man came up to him and, kneeling before him, said, "Lord, have mercy on my son, for he is an epileptic and he suffers terribly. For often he falls into the fire, and often into the water. And I brought him to your disciples, and they could not heal him." And Jesus answered, "O faithless and twisted generation, how long am I to be with you? How long am I to bear with you? Bring him here to me." And Jesus rebuked the demon, and it came out of him, and the boy was healed instantly.

This shows us that the disease epilepsy is a sickness, and when the person was under the control of this spirit, they did things they would not normally do, such as falling in fire or water, as the son of the man did above. It could be other things the person does when they are under the control of a spirit. Also, from the above sickness, it shows it was actually a demon that was causing this sickness. Finally, Jesus said, "How long am I to be with you?" He meant, in order for them to move in the healing and delivering power, He needed to be with them. This shows us that people of God that move today with this power, however, the spirit may not come out immediately as it did with Jesus; it may be a longer process... but with determination, faith and being prayerful, you will get the deliverance required.

Read another deliverance miracle Jesus did in Mark 5: 1 – 20:

They came to the other side of the sea, to the country of the Gerasenes. And when Jesus had stepped out of the boat, immediately there met him out of the tombs a man with an unclean spirit. He lived among the tombs. And no one could bind him anymore, not even with a chain, for he had often been bound with shackles and chains, but he wrenched the chains apart, and he broke the shackles in pieces. No one had the strength to subdue him. Night and day among the tombs and on the mountains he was always crying out and cutting himself with stones.

Again we see another example of a man with a demon possessing his life to the point where he was so strong that no-one could bind him anymore. So many times people that have an unusual strength; one should question where this strength comes from. This demon also made him do things such as live in places where there was no community, amongst the dead, and he used to cut himself. Many times we see people that have tendencies to cut themselves or worship the dead or spend their time speaking with the dead. This is not normal, and you need to ask yourself what demon is operating in the person's life.

Hence, from the above examples, we see people that were afflicted by illnesses, and their minds were also afflicted. It can be in many forms and, by being a deliverance minister and pastor, I have seen people being set free from many different spirits. Jesus talked about some of these spirits above in the passages discussed.

You may be asking me how these spirits gained access in the first place... well, I believe it is mainly through two reasons: generational sin and personal sin. For example, your father and grandfather may have had a spirit of adultery and now you are compelled to do the same. Your mother may have had a spirit of sickness and now that same sickness is upon you... this all needs to be broken by the name of Jesus and by His blood that was shed on the cross 2,000 years ago for your freedom. Remember you were bought with a price... the sacrifice of the son of God. He paid the price for you and I to be free from bondage... suffer no more in Jesus' name and be set free!

Chapter 2
How can I be set free?

Firstly, you need to be in a church that moves with the deliverance anointing. There are many churches around but very few actually believe or even fewer practise deliverance… it is very sad that, in the body of Christ today, as Christians we do not practise a vital part of what Jesus said in Matthew 10: 8: *"Heal the sick, raise the dead, cure those with leprosy, and* **cast out demons.***"*

Once you have found a church that believes in deliverance, stay in the church and learn about deliverance. Approach the ministers about deliverance if they haven't approached you yet and inform them that you would like to go through deliverance.

Ensure that everything in your life is right before you take this serious step. Here are some points to think about:

1. Have you been baptised in water after you have repented and accepted Christ as your Personal Saviour?

2. Are you committed to spending time daily with the Lord such as praying, reading the word and repenting of your sins?

3. Will you be committed in attending church and being under the covering of men and women of God that move in the anointing?

4. Will you be obedient to the Word of God and to pastors or ministers in your church?

5. Finally, are you willing to make the <u>commitment of living right?</u>

The reason I am pointing these factors out to you is that many want to come for deliverance, but they are not fully committed; then, when they start the deliverance process, and the battle is too much for them, they tend to leave the church, and even Christianity, as Satan will fight to keep his hold on their life. Once you start deliverance, there will be a battle. This battle may consist of the some or all of the following:

1. Doubt whether or not to continue with your deliverance
2. To stay in the church which is delivering you
3. People around you will start attacking you either verbally or even physically
4. There will definitely be a battle in your mind
5. Attacks will come from places you won't expect
6. Being under deception, thinking that you have been completely delivered after a few sessions

Many start deliverance but, due to them not being strong in the Lord, they lose their faith when the battle gets too hard and give up too easily. This is where you need to be strong and continue the good fight, and God will give you the grace and strength to continue, no matter how hard it is. Some people ask how long deliverance takes to happen; there is no definite answer, as it will depend on your willingness to serve and obey God, live right and be committed to attending all deliverance sessions... until a man or woman of God informs you that you can stop. This is a process, and can take some time, but persevere through it and the benefits of deliverance are awesome!

These benefits include the following:

Obviously, you will no longer be under the affliction of demons disturbing your physical, emotional and mental health, as you will have been set free! You will feel that freedom in your mind and body; people around you will even notice how different you look once you have been through deliverance! I remember that, when I was completing my own deliverance, many people mentioned how my face looked much better and different! Isn't that awesome that spiritual freedom can even bring these physical changes?

Spiritually, you will be able to spend more time with the Lord, pray more and read His word. You will be able to feel His presence and get His guidance clearly on areas in your life and others. You will be able to enjoy spending time with believers and reading or listening to Christian material. There won't be demons in you fighting every time you try to pick up and read the Word or any other Christian material.

You will notice an overall improvement in simple things in your life like doing your job, driving, speaking, *etc.* You will notice that deliverance helps you in all areas of your life.

Finally, and most importantly, you will be filled and empowered with the Holy Spirit to do many works for Him; there won't be spirits blocking your spiritual antennae in doing the work of God. You will be cleaned up (pure), and the Lord will be able to use you for His glory. You will be able to pray for people without fearing that the spirits you have are being transferred to others. You will move more and more in power to complete the ministry given to you and to fulfil the Great Commission which is to preach the gospel, heal the sick and cast out demons.

These are some of the many benefits of deliverance. I noticed such a change in my mind and circumstances around me when I started deliverance sessions, and realised I would not have gotten so far spiritually and physically if I hadn't made the choice of going through my own deliverance. I think many Christians want the quick and easy way to get into their callings and ministry and are not willing to go through a process: part of that process is deliverance. How can they expect to fulfil the calling and destiny of their lives without doing all that God requires, part of which is deliverance? Yes, I understand it is not easy, it is time-consuming, it is a process, but think of where you will be in two to five years, once you have been through deliverance? You will be more able to do the work of God – He is calling you, and many areas you have been struggling with will literally disappear with deliverance! And yes, you must at all times LIVE RIGHT to maintain your deliverance, of which we will speak in more detail below.

Are you ready to experience change? Yes?

Okay, so you are ready, you have put everything in place and are willing to go through the fight of being set free and maintaining your deliverance. That is wonderful to know! Hence you can approach a deliverance ministry and go to their daily or weekly deliverance sessions. Some churches may do this on a one-on-one basis and other churches may have group deliverance sessions. You may feel embarrassed in a group session, but Jesus' ministry was public and when he delivered people, it was open for everyone to see. Before you go to deliverance, be aware that you may see all sorts of things, such as people coughing, screaming, rolling on the floor, yawning, vomiting, *etc*. You see, when Jesus commanded sprits to come out, some came out by jerking and screaming, as the Bible says. This is the way Jesus delivered people.

Others may say that deliverance is just repenting and saying a prayer and you are free. This is false teaching, as this is not the way Jesus Christ of Nazareth did deliverance. If it was so simple, then why did not Jesus, the son of the Almighty God, do so? The Bible says to cast out demons. When I was going through deliverance, a well-known woman came to preach about deliverance at a conference, so we all eagerly went to hear what she had to say. She got all the people in the congregation to anoint themselves with oil, repent and pray that all demons leave. She then said to us all that we are free – in one evening. I knew this was not the case: neither I nor the others I was with felt free, and when we stepped into deliverance a few days later, spirits were cast out of our lives. So this was major deception at the meeting. How sad to deceive people of God in this manner, thinking they were all set free. The preacher herself was probably under this great deception without even realising it.

So there are different ways a spirit can manifest before it comes out. Please do not mock or laugh when you enter a deliverance session, as that spirit can easily come in you: it is always looking for a body to inhabit.

Another way of being set free is through selfdeliverance; this can be done in the following ways:

1. **Read scriptures on deliverance –**

   The Bible has many scriptures on deliverance, use a concordance and allocate the scriptures you want to use for your own personal war towards spirits inhabiting parts of your life. For instance, "you have the power to trample over serpents and scorpions".

2. **Start worshipping and praising God –**

   Some good worship music may help you in worshipping the Lord if you are not used to this. Try to find worship music that is more warfare-based; this will help your faith as well when going into warfare.

3. **Spend time repenting of your sins and the sins of your forefathers –**

   How many times do we actually repent as Christians, maybe once every so often….? Actually, Jesus says every time we pray we should ask the Lord to forgive us from our sins. This is in the Lord's Prayer. Also, pray that, whatever sins your forefathers did, they too will be forgiven in Jesus' name, as their sins may affect you up to the third and fourth generation (according to Exodus 34: 7).

4. **Cover yourself and your family with the blood of Jesus –**

   This is very important, because many times a spirit can leave you and go to another member of your family if there is an open door in the spiritual realm, for example, through sin.

5. **Ask the Lord to deliver you, to set you free –**

   Be specific in what spirits inhabit your life: you may be addicted to smoking, so ask the Lord to deliver you from this spirit. You may want to draw a list of spirits you think you may have and ask God to deal with each one specifically. Even call these by name, *ie.* "I command the spirit of sickness and disease to leave my body". I discuss more of the types of spirits there are in other chapters within this book.

6. **Command spirits to leave your life in the name of Jesus** –

   Be bold and do not be afraid to command demons out of your life in the name of Jesus. This is spiritual warfare, for (as it says in Ephesians 6: 12), we do not wrestle against flesh and blood, but against principalities, against powers, against the rulers of the darkness of this age, against spiritual *hosts* of wickedness in the heavenly *places*. So we need to "wrestle" with these forces in the spirit commanding them to leave in Jesus' name. The Bible says that "when you have faith as small as a mustard seed, you can say to this mountain to be thrown into the sea and it will". So why not demons? Have faith and command, as you have been given authority to trample over serpents and scorpions, as it says in Luke 10: 19.

7. **Be forceful when doing this and command them to come out by coughing or vomiting, etc.** –

   Don't give up and if nothing is happening; check yourself, are you living right? Is there any fear in you that may be stopping your deliverance? Do not listen to the lies of the Devil that there is nothing there.

8. **If you feel nothing is happening, then go on a dry fast for 12 – 24 hours, asking the Lord to start the delivering process** –

   Sometimes, for deliverance to start effectively, this is what is required. When the apostles were trying to command demons to leave a person's life and it wasn't going, Jesus said that these only go through fasting and prayer (Mark 9: 29). Keep on doing this until you start feeling something is happening… when you start going through deliverance. Also, ensure you are living right, as sometimes God will not start this in your life if you have not put your house in order spiritually.

9. When the spirits start coming out or you feel like something is happening, do not stop: continue until you see or feel something has left you. Many times they will come out coughing, shouting or even vomiting, so prepare yourself for this.

10. When you have finished, ask the Holy Spirit to fill every area that a spirit has left in Jesus' name, and for Him to cover you and your family with the blood of Jesus again.

11. Finally, ensure you continue living right no matter what the consequence is. Remember, Satan will try to tempt you into sin so he can get access to your body again.

Deliverance is a process and you need to continue deliverance for a period of time as not all spirits will instantly leave you. Sometimes you may be attending deliverance for 24 months and, even then, you will not be completely free… but you would have been set free in many areas in your life. Also, I would highly recommend you attend group deliverance sessions on a weekly basis, as this will ensure a man or woman of God will be able to identify spirits still there, motivate and encourage you in the deliverance process. Some people say they are through with deliverance after a few weeks or months and that they have been delivered. When this happens, the Devil has clearly deceived them, as it's not as easy and as quick as that.

There was one woman once who was desperate for deliverance due to coming from a background that worshipped false gods. When she started attending deliverance, the woman was manifesting a lot and there were so many spirits there. I encouraged this lady to continue with her deliverance, but after a couple of weeks she said she was completely free and decided she didn't need deliverance anymore. I knew that there was a spirit of deception operating and was sad for her as I could see that she was still manifesting very much. However, it was her choice, despite the discussions I had with her regarding that her deliverance wasn't finished yet. About a year later, the same lady contacted me informing me of the many problems plaguing her life; things had even gotten worse than before because she had started deliverance, but had not finished it, and there were many spirits still there! It was a shame to see this happen, but she had made a choice to leave before her deliverance had ended.

You may be asking me how one would know they are no longer under the oppression of a spirit. The answer is quite simple: when commanding that spirit to leave, is it still manifesting? Another way you know a spirit has left you is that you feel it leaving you: you actually feel a force going and you know that you know that you know it is gone. Finally, you will know yourself by the fruit you are bearing. For example, if you had a spirit of addiction to smoking and you feel that you need to smoke after going through deliverance (and the craving is forceful to the point that you cannot help yourself), then you know that there is still a spirit operating. However, remember how cunning and deceiving spirits are and they will try everything they possibly can to gain access back into your life and hence they will tempt you uncontrollably. It is essential you do not go back to it, as once you do, then you have again opened the doors for these demons to come back with bigger spirits of addiction! Be warned and take this seriously.

Chapter 3
How do I maintain my deliverance?

Jesus says the following in Luke 11: 24 – 26:
"When an evil spirit leaves a person, it goes into the desert, searching for rest. But when it finds none, it says, 'I will return to the person I came from.' So it returns and finds that its former home is all swept and in order. Then the spirit finds seven other spirits more evil than itself, and they all enter the person and live there. And so that person is worse off than before."

This shows us that spirits, once they are commanded out of a person, can return. However, they return with more powerful spirits and the person is worse off than before. A word of caution here: deliverance is not to be taken lightly; it is not for Christians who are not committed to the things of God and live in sin. Every man or woman of God must warn their congregations about the seriousness of deliverance and the importance of maintaining their freedom. I have seen Christians who have decided to attend deliverance but, due to their lack of commitment, have gone back into their worldly desires and the spirits have come back doubled. It is scary when you see how people become if they do not maintain their deliverance. Some people do this all the time... being in and out of deliverance due to falling into temptation and sin. So, as a Christian, you must take a stand if you are to be delivered: a stand in following Christ, being obedient to the word, being in an anointed place and being under a rightful spiritual covering... and striving to do what is right, no matter what the cost.

Being under a rightful spiritual covering is being under anointed men or women of God that the Lord has led you to for deliverance or to be mentored by. As it says in Hebrews 13, they were given to you by God as your spiritual authority. They must be blameless, living holy and pure lives, serving the Lord with all their heart. Many times we are under leaders who have not undergone deliverance, and if that person prays for you, then their spirits may be transferred onto you. Therefore, the Bible says you will know them "by their fruit" – on the way they live for Jesus and the anointing that moves upon their lives. Many times we are too eager to allow people to lay their hands on us and pray for us, but what do you know about that person and the fruit they are displaying? Churches which are led by the Spirit of God will always ensure that holy and righteous people are placed in the rightful positions to pray for people and when they pray, demons will flee, healing both physical and emotional will take place and the gospel will be preached. Zachariah 4:6 says, *"Not by might, nor by power, but by my Spirit, says the Lord of Hosts."*

If you have made a commitment to undergo deliverance, then find a local deliverance ministry to attend if the one you are not attending does not move in deliverance. But remember demons will try anything they can to get back into you through the following areas:

a. Sin
b. Evil Dreams
c. Emotions such as Fear, Anger, Jealousy *etc.*
d. Senses – Hear and see
e. Witchcraft sent to you (or any occultist movement you were involved in)
f. Spoken Curses
g. Generational Curses

h. Negative Words

i. Disobedience

Let's talk a little more about these areas:

Sin

Sin is anything the Bible says not to do…have a look at the Ten Commandments, have a look at Leviticus and have a look at what Jesus says. Sin can be gossiping, lying, stealing, promiscuity, fornication, adultery, other sexual sins and sexual perversions. Hence, any time you fall into sin, instantly you have broken a Biblical law and the price will be paid through a spirit gaining access into your life.

However, you may argue with me, saying you are only human, and yes – that is what the Bible tells us in Romans 3: 23 (*"all have sinned and fallen short of the glory of God"*). Nonetheless, we need to be quick to repent, asking the Lord to forgive us and close the spiritual doors and seal them with the Blood of Jesus that may be an entry point to the devil.

Remember that the Old Testament represents the spiritual realm and the New Testament represents the physical realm for us Christians. So, if the Israelites did that, how much more we should do it on a daily basis? As Christians we have been born again, so we are spiritually (re)born. Hence, there are two lives in one body: our soul and our spirit. Our spirit wars against devils in the spiritual realm, sometimes you may see what is going on when the Lord opens your spiritual eyes (for example, you will see visions or even hear and smell things). The Old Testament represents our spiritual lives, for example, when the Israelites go to war against the Jebusites,

Amalakites, Moabites, *etc.* to get them out of their land, that is what we do in spirit: we go to war against devils inhabiting our spiritual land and command them to leave. When we do this, we will actually notice things move and change for us in the physical!

The New Testament teaches us how to live in the physical, for example, what Jesus says in Mark 12:31, "love your neighbour as you love yourself". Now, many people don't understand the differences between the Old and New Testaments, and often will criticise the Bible, saying it is contradicting itself. But, actually, the Old Testament concerns the Spirit, and the New Testament the physical realm (flesh), as they are both living in ONE body. I have often noticed Christians that just do what the New Testament says in living our daily lives. Christians walking in the physical are just living only half of their Christian life; they are not living it in full! And, many times, what I have noticed with these Christians is that their lives are stagnant: they are facing many challenges and are unable to cope with day-to-day circumstances as they are not exercising the full authority given to us by God and that is by taking authority in the spirit and commanding any spiritual Hittite, Moabite, Jebusite, Philistine to leave our lives in the spirit!

However, the Christians that live both parts of their walk with Jesus both in the Spirit and in the Physical, *ie.*, exercising both the Old and New Testaments by loving people in the physical and going to war against demons in the spiritual, live victorious lives and overcome with much ease any of the challenges Satan brings to them! This is done by exercising their dominion given to Man in the earthly plane and going to war daily on anything they notice in the spiritual.

Maria Yiangou

Emotions

The Lord continued to show me that there are different entry points. For example, you may open a door to fear. So how would one go about getting that out after being through deliverance? Again the Lord showed me the following: remember when the Israelites drove out the Amalekites, the Canaanites and Moabites, *etc.?* So we, too, must ask the Holy Spirit to drive out our spiritual Moabites, Amalekites and Canaanites, such as the spirits of fear, anger, jealousy, lust and so forth. Remember, we then close the door and seal it with the blood of Jesus. Every time you notice something is creeping into your life, then drive it out in Jesus' name!

Senses

Sight and hearing can open doors to spirits too. Sight can be anything you watch that is impure. There is so much on our TV screens, advertisements and even the Internet, and if we are not careful and self-censor what we open our eyes to, we can easily open a door to a spirit. How many times have you heard people watching horror films and then start having fears and nightmares? This is not normal: there is a spirit that is oppressing that person and he/she needs to command it out of their life in Jesus' name. The same thing goes for hearing music, lyrics, and people around us, for that too will have an impact on our lives. For instance, if you are constantly around people speaking profanities or hearing lyrics using foul language, you will open a door to a spirit of profanity and will not be able to help yourself speaking swear words either out loud or in your mind. Hence, as a pastor, I would greatly encourage you to be careful of what you read or listen to, so that you do not open doors. Many times, I have noticed people listening to oppressive news or watching oppressive images and they start feeling depressed: it is due to what they are feeding their eyes and ears with. The Bible says, in Ephesians 5: 19, to "speak to each other with psalms and hymns, making melody in our hearts to the Lord". In Colossians 3: 16 it says to "let the word of the Messiah inhabit you richly with wisdom and teaching" …This shows us the importance of listening to Godly music, Godly talk, and reading the Bible. This shows how important it is to surround ourselves with Godliness consistently. For example, in your car, listen to Worship music; at home, listen to the Bible when cooking; watch Christian television and innocent programmes. Ensure your atmosphere is filled with media that is pleasing to God and you will notice how you, too, will feel encouraged, blessed, and able to overcome any of life circumstances easily, as this is what you are filling your mind with.

Evil Dreams

I would advise anyone reading this book not to take dreams lightly as they, too, stand as an entry point to the demonic realm! I have seen so many bad things happen to people once they have had bad dreams. For example, seeing a snake battling with you in the dream signifies Satan has planned a physical enemy to battle with you in the physical. Therefore, should evil dreams happen at night, it is crucial you get up in the morning and destroy them in the name of Jesus, covering your life, family, and any other areas in your life with the blood of Jesus! I would suggest you continue destroying such a dream for three to seven days to ensure it is completely destroyed. Do not take such dreams lightly as they will manifest in the physical and bring problems to your life, as they are entry points in the physical realm.

Dreams can also be good and used by God to speak to you and show you situations regarding your life. For example, Jacob's dream at Bethel when the Lord spoke to him about the land He was giving Jacob (Genesis 28: 10 – 17)

Therefore, I always recommend the following before you go to bed at night: ask the Lord to give you dreams and speak to you. Ask the Lord to close all doors to the enemy trying to inject you with evil dreams in Jesus' name.

Witchcraft And Occultist Involvement

Witchcraft and ANY Occult involvement is a huge topic; however, I will briefly touch upon it in this book. Like many Christians, I did not believe this existed and, if it did, I foolishly thought it could not harm me. Witchcraft cannot touch you if you apply certain steps in your life. Being a Pastor of a Deliverance Ministry, I have seen many Christians battling with witchcraft being sent to them and, when delivering them, they always get the victory! This is real, and it does affect Christians today, but you can be delivered from any spirit of witchcraft. Do not fear witchcraft, but be ready to fight it.

In this book I will mainly contend that it is real and another entry point Satan uses through people, his agents (witches and warlocks), to destroy lives. Usually, people who use evil spirits to send to others are initiated, and many times they are compelled to send evil spirits to people, whether they know them or not. The Lord showed me not to hate witches, but to understand they are under a spirit when they do this act. Hence we need to continually bind the demon of witchcraft in them, and this will stop them sending witchcraft to you. Satan will use this as another entry point. And remember it is not up to us to take vengeance upon these people as the Lord tells us in Romans 12: 19 *("Vengeance is mine, sayeth the Lord.")* Just bind the spirit in them in Jesus' name.

Curses

Another entry point in a person's life for spirits to have access is through curses. This could be you cursing yourself, or this may be someone else cursing you. Curses are very powerful when the person has been wronged or curses you under anger. Hence this is another doorway Satan uses to come into your life and cause destruction. Curses can be broken through deliverance, fasting and prayer, moving in covenants for very powerful curses, and taking part in a special day called the Day of Passover.

There was a particular breakthrough I had been trying to get for a time and the Lord showed me a vision of my grandmother on the mountain cursing the family. I remember I called my spiritual father in the Lord and told him about the vision, as I was still young in the things of spiritual warfare. He explained to me that it was very hard to break this curse and, in his words, *"it will take Heaven to break this."* However, I knew the God I served, and I would do anything to break it off my life. The Lord instructed me to start going to midnight services: at the time, I didn't know why on Earth I needed to wake up at 3*am* to go to a service... but I was obedient. Within a short space of time, at one of the 3am services, I broke this curse, and within a month I received my miracle!

Do not underestimate the power of praying in the third or fourth watch! Look at what happened in Acts 16, when Apostle Paul and Silas were praying at midnight. The

Bible says that, as they were praying and singing hymns to God, there was a massive earthquake, the prison doors flew open and the chains fell off the prisoners! Imagine that, just by getting together and praying and worshipping God at midnight, there is power in the name of Jesus for every bondage, curse and generational curse to be broken off your life! Why midnight? Well, I believe there is power when you sacrifice one of the things you dearly love, and that is sleep – something has to happen by force when praying at this hour! I have seen miracle after miracle in people's lives when they fast and come to midnight services. No bondage can stay in your life when you follow praying at night and fasting too!

Generational Curses

This is another area of ways in which evil spirits can enter your life and have a hold on the following in your life:

- Promotion
- Success
- Poverty
- Health
- Marriage
- Mental well-being

Generational curses are evil acts, sins that our forefathers have committed, *eg.* our parents, grandparents and our great-grandparents. The Bible says, in Exodus 34: 7, that God will punish us to the third and fourth generation. You may say this is the Old Testament, but Jesus says in the New Testament that He did not come to put away the Old Testament but to fulfil it (Matthew 5: 17)!

Hence, from this, generational curses are real and they can come upon your life from the sins your ancestors have committed such as murder, witchcraft, idolatry, praying to false gods, sexual perversions and so forth. In Leviticus 18, the Bible talks about the many types of sexual sins there are, and not to do these, as there is a price to pay and, yes, even to the third and fourth generation you may be paying a price for the sins your ancestors committed.

I was born with an incurable disease and, from a young age, I had to be taking medication every day to keep the symptoms under control. My secondcousins and third-cousins had the same disease and they, too, had to be taking medication. I visited doctors in three different countries seeking cures, but nothing could be done. One day a man of God was praying for me and explained to me where this sin had come from. He actually explained that an ancestor of mine had done a particular sexual sin and that is why all the second and third cousins were suffering from this. Thinking back to my ancestors, this practise was easily done and hence the problem we were now all facing. Finally, there was an explanation to this... and, nine months later, I received my healing and have been free ever since. It was not the result of my sin, or an error of mine, that opened a door to this incurable disease but from a forefather of mine that I had never even met! Thank God for His mercy and love on our lives that we can be set free even from incurable diseases in the name of Jesus!

I can hear you saying that it is not fair; I believe the Lord did this to warn people against doing these sins. However, their disobedience brings about generational curses. And those who obey the Bible, it says in Exodus 34:

7 that their children will reap God's goodness for a thousand generations! As a Pastor, I have noticed that when people come from parents and grandparents of strong and focused believers in the Lord, they seem to have it easier in getting their breakthroughs. However, those of us that come from unbelieving backgrounds into the Kingdom of God have to battle much more in getting our miracles. But the good thing is that there is an answer to all of this, and that is Jesus. Through the power of deliverance and being in a place where the anointing moves, it will break every yoke, according to Isaiah 10: 27.

Negative Words

These are words that people are speaking over your life such as *'she will never get married'* or *'she will die an old maid'* or *'she will remain on the shelf'*, etc. These are ALL negative words and spirits can attach themselves to negative words and, hence, breakthrough in marriage will never come until you know you are dealing with this spirit and you break it in Jesus' name. Many times I hear believers speaking upon themselves negatively; you need to stop this immediately, as the Bible says there is power in the tongue (Proverbs 18: 21) and what you are speaking will come to pass through a spirit entering an open door in this area.

I will give you an example of what happened to me. I was very young at the time and I went for my driving test and failed miserably! After that, people started speaking negatively, laughing at my expense in regards to driving. One person in particular would speak very negatively in regards to my driving, but I never took much notice and each time I would go for my test, I would fail. One evening, before my fifth attempt, I cried out to the Lord, and instantly the Lord spoke to me about the spirit of negative words. I immediately commanded it to leave and that moment I was delivered from the spirit. The next day I went for my test and passed with ease! I cannot explain the joy and happiness I felt: it took me six years to achieve this, and all because there was a spirit of negative words in operation!

Do not even let others speak about you negatively, even in a joking manner; do not entertain such words against your life. Once the Holy Spirit has shown you or you have discerned a spirit of negative words, then you need to take authority in the name of Jesus and prohibit it from operating in your life. Do not put up with this spirit any longer.

If somebody says something negative about you, your family members, or any other area in your life, immediately use these phrases:

- I reject that word over my life no in Jesus' name
- I rebuke that word in Jesus' name; it will never come to pass in my life!

The Key to Maintaining your Deliverance is this: Ensure on a daily basis you spend time with the Lord by praying and asking the precious Holy Spirit to come upon you with his presence and His anointing. Be in the Lord's presence when you are praying, daily. Don't just pray and go about your *daily* life but spend time in **_His presence._**

It will take time for you to get into the presence of God but with perseverance you will accomplish this. His presence is sweet and satisfying; you will notice the joy, peace and happiness upon you when you spend time in His presence. Don't be in a rush to leave the presence of God or to just say a quick prayer in the morning. Because when you open doors through sin; even sin that is minor in your eyes, these are still doorways for spirits to enter. But when you are in the presence on a daily basis, no spirit can enter your life and thus you are maintaining the deliverance you have received!

Make time for Jesus, maybe you cannot pray in the morning due to early shift, you can pray in the evening or even better wake up earlier than you do and spend time in His presence. I find praying early hours in the morning the best, as there are no distractions i.e. phones ringing, e-mails sent, doorbells ringing etc. Just quietness and hence it is easier for you to get quiet and in the spirit. Ask the Lord as you do for you to enter His presence and for Him to come upon you in Jesus name.

Chapter 4
What other ways can demons enter your life?

There are many spirits that can inhabit a person and this can be seen when Jesus asked the spirit who he was and the demon replied, *"My name is Legion, for we are many"* (Mark 5: 9). This shows that there can be many spirits inhabiting a person and, depending on how many doors the person has opened, even more demons can enter that person. Doors can be opened by methods mentioned above, such as curses, sin, negative words, witchcraft... and even tattoos, idols of gods, items from foreign countries that have been blessed by priests of other religions, yoga, acupuncture, cultural dances, *etc*.

In regards to tattoos and idols of other gods, the Bible is clear as to not have any marks on the body (Leviticus 19: 28) and to not worship other gods. When people are doing these things, they are disobeying the word of God, and this opens doors to spirits. You are giving these spirits a legal right to enter your life when you are disobeying the word of God. The same goes for yoga and ancient or cultural dances which, in the old days, would symbolise worship to a god in their religion; by doing that dance, instantly you are worshipping unknowingly a foreign god, and this opens doors in the supernatural realm.

I was teaching a class once, as I was a Teacher / College Lecturer by profession. Part of the lesson was for trainee teachers to do a micro-teach (which is basically to teach the class something for fifteen minutes as practise). One of the trainee teachers decided to teach the class a cultural dance, which seemed very exciting and interesting. When the young lady was teaching the dance, I noticed all these strange movements, but didn't think anything of it. Later that evening, I walked into the classroom and immediately discerned there was a spirit in the room. I didn't know what was in there and enquired from the Lord; He immediately showed me the dance was actually a worship dance to one of her gods and that gave legal ground for a spirit to enter that classroom. I immediately prayed over the room and anointed it with oil, commanding every evil spirit to leave, and it did. The peace in that room was instantly restored! The bible says that God's people are destroyed because lack of knowledge (Hosea 4: 6). Let us understand the supernatural realm so we can protect ourselves from anything that can contaminate our lives.

Even bringing items home from countries which are not Christian may be an open door to the supernatural door; those items may have been blessed by a priest of a false god, who may bring a spirit into your home as they are not worshipping the true God, but a false god which is a demon. As believers we have to be mindful of all these items, as the demon world seek to enter a body by all means possible, and when you give them legal ground, they will easily do this.

There was a lady that told me her father's friend had brought a statue from Africa as a gift, and soon afterwards, everything in the family started falling apart, such as the man's business and his marriage. This statue was definitely a door to this man's house in the spirit without them knowing. It gave the legal right for a spirit to come into the family home and cause chaos; it was used as a point of contact for destruction upon that man's household. As Christians we go to foreign places on holiday, and bring back many different articles, but many times these articles represent a god or have been 'prayed' for by priests who do not serve the real God and these items give access to spirits in the supernatural realm to come into your home. It is the same as having images of people that a particular religion may worship; this is all idol-worship and opens doors into your family home.

As born-again believers we need to know exactly what we bring into our homes. There was a secondhand book I had once ordered online on Christianity and, as soon as this book came into my home, I felt a human spirit astral projecting into my home. At first I thought that this couldn't be; however, my husband saw in the spirit another human spirit moving in our home. Instantly, I knew that the book was a doorway, spiritually, for these human spirits to come into our home, so I immediately got rid of the book, then we prayed over our home and anointed it with oil. Everything went back to normal, no more human spirits astral projecting into our home. It was a shame that they used a Christian book to gain access, but they can use anything as a point of contact into your home, so be careful what comes into your house.

As you can see from the above example, it is not just demonic spirits that we have to deal with, but also human spirits that are used by Satan to cause chaos in people's lives when they astral project into your home. However, these spirits cannot inhabit your life (as they have their own body) but they are used by Satan for other purposes.

The same goes for the use of tarot cards, reading coffee cups, wearing the evil eye for protection, visiting a fortune teller, reading your star signs (astrology), eating foods sacrificed to idols... they are all means of doorways being opened and spirits entering. Having been a pastor and a deliverance minister, many times has the Lord showed me areas people have sinned in by opening doors without even realising they have. I have said, in deliverance, one should repent for reading coffee cups or tarot cards, *etc.*, and as soon as the person has repented, the spirit comes out coughing, screaming or vomiting. The person would then sometimes come up to me after deliverance and confess about their involvement in any of the above activities. Hence, this shows how the above demonic activities do open doors so, as Bible-believing Christians, we must stay away from all these areas and keep ourselves pure. The Bible says that the only way to see God is if we are pure (Matthew 5: 8)!

Search your home today to see if you have anything that may be from the occult and throw it out. Also, see if you have any idols or images of gods. These all need to be thrown out, as God does not tolerate disobedience (Exodus 20: 5)! As a pastor, I have noticed people who have pictures of dead people and other gods in their house, praying to these idols; they usually suffer from a spirit of sickness and disease. Repent for having it in your home and your involvement in it. Then, with anointed oil, go around your home commanding every spirit to leave your house; anoint all doors, windows and walls with the oil, and invite the Lord's presence in your home today.

Chapter 5
What types of Spirits are there?

There are many types of demons and I will briefly group some of them so that you can recognise them more easily. Demons are associated with one another and usually there is one strong man and many smaller demons under that one demon. An example of this is when Jesus asked the demon what his name was and he replied "Legion, for we are many" (Mark 5: 9). For instance, there may be a spirit of anger, and with that spirit there will be jealousy, revenge, rage and suicide within the same person. Also, you will notice that in a person who has – for instance – the spirit of lust, then that person usually has a number of other spirits attached to it, such as masturbation, pornography, adultery and so forth. It is very sad to see a person who is happily married turn to pornography or adultery due to the problem of lust in that person's life. How much heartache would be spared in marriages if these spirits were recognised and cast out from the beginning, instead of discovering the problem in the midst or at the end of the marriage? Therefore, the majority of the problems behind a person's life are due to demonic oppression; if we are able to recognize the issues and the spirits attached to these, then we will become victorious in combatting and dealing with the spirits behind the problem... and we would be, as the Bible says, MORE THAN CONQUERORS!

As demons travel in legions, I will group them so you understand what types of demons are in a legion.

But before we go onto that you may be asking: what is a legion? In Roman times, the Roman army was divided into legions. Every legion had a name and each would attack different tribes, groups or people. A legion could consist of between 4,000 and 6,000 men!

So when Jesus asked the demon who he was, he replied, "Legion, for we are many."

In the spirit world there could be many similar demons and, also, a mixed variety of demons, depending on the doors the person has opened in the supernatural realm.

Spirit Of Anger

The Spirit of Anger can have any of the following demons attached to it: Murder, Hate, Rage, Violence, Death, Revenge, Destruction, Suicide, Abortion, Jealousy, Fighting and so forth. You will usually notice that an angry person will take revenge, will try to destroy things around them, and may be very violent. When someone with a spirit of anger is going through deliverance, it is important to have two people casting this demon out, as many times the spirit will manifest, and will be uncontrollable in the person you are commanding it to leave from.

Occultist Spirit

Occult Demons can have any of the following spirits attached to it: Medium and Fortune-Telling, Coffee Cup Reading, Tea Leaf Reading, Palm Reading, Crystal Ball Gazing, Tarot Cards, Ouija Boards, Séances, Astrology, Hypnotism, editation, Crystals, Witchcraft, Satanism, Voodoo, Channeling, Reincarnation, Astral Projection, Necromancy, New Age Movement techniques and activities such as yoga, chanting and so forth. A person that starts reading coffee cups, tea leaves will usually move to something else within this area, eg. tarot cards. Every time they try to stay away from this, they just can't; it is like a drug that continually brings them back to doing any of the above and more. Hence, when someone starts with something 'light', they will tend to move into stronger areas within the above; the more they get entangled, the harder it is for them to know Jesus as their Personal Saviour, or to go through deliverance, as they have most probably been initiated.

Sexual Spirits

Sexual demons have a huge hold over many people's lives and these are the many demons that can inhabit people that are involved with sexual sins: Lust, Fornication, Divorce, Adultery, Masturbation, Pornography, Paedophilia, Rape, Incest, Sexual Orgies, Prostitution, Soul Ties, Bestiality, Sadomasochism, Sexual Perversions, spiritual husbands and wives, and so forth. The Bible is clear in many areas not to commit sexual sins, but many Christians have this hidden, and continue despite Biblical warnings (Leviticus 18). They are too ashamed to let their pastors know the problem, and they are suffering in silence. When they are not in a deliverance ministry, and it is not dealt with through these spirits being cast out, they will end up leaving the church… and even backsliding as they have been overcome by the power of this spirit! It is such a shame to see how these spirits can have such an effect on people's lives. It doesn't shock me any more when people in prominent positions have committed adultery, or another sin, as there are spirits in that person and – if they are not dealt with – it may ultimately lead them astray.

Pride And Jezebel

The demons of Pride and Jezebel have the following spirits usually associated with them: Pride, Arrogance, Rebellion, Blasphemy, Control, Domination, Intimidation, Manipulation, Possessiveness, Contention, Quarreling, Criticism, Judgement, Selfishness, Unbelief and Doubt, Scepticism, Greed, Paranoia, Deceit, Mockery and so forth.

Pride is a very dangerous spirit to have, as the Bible says in James 5: 1–20 that God opposes the proud, which means that whatever you try to do, God himself will oppose you. It is very important to examine yourself and ask the Lord to humble you and deliver you from the spirit of pride, as God will never use a vessel that is proud. Look what happened to King Saul, the first King of Israel, because of his pride! This is a spirit, and needs to be dealt with very quickly if you are to move in the calling that the Lord has for your life. I will talk about Jezebel in much more detail in the next chapter. I feel like writing a book about this spirit, as so many churches and people of God have been stung by the spirit of Jezebel, and even destroyed due to this demon. One thing I will say now is that the Bible says in Revelation 2: 20 *not to tolerate this spirit!* It is time we wake up to this spirit and, if you feel you have Jezebel, then you need serious deliverance as wherever you go this spirit will use you to destroy churches, the anointing, the power of God and people of God. This spirit in particular fights people of God, usually moves as a so called 'prophetess' and will make people believe everything she says is the truth when she prophesises, dreams she sees and what she feels the Lord is telling her. This is all deception used to ultimately deceive and destroy the church. Jezebels will always fight male prophets in particular, and I have seen this happen, but true prophets and people of God will know what spirit they are dealing with. *The key is not to come under the influence of the Jezebel spirit and to bind the demon in operation.*

Spirit Of Madness

The demon of Madness encompasses the following spirits: Fear, Depression, Torment, Dread, Hopelessness, Despair, Insecurity, Paranoia, Suspicion, Distrust, Insecurity, Loneliness, Shyness, Discouragement, Lying, Deceit, Antisocial, Obsessive Behaviour, Phobias, Madness, Insanity, Schizophrenia, Multiple Personalities, Hearing Voices and so forth. Many times this demon comes into a person's life from occultist involvement, curses, generational curses and witchcraft. However, when these demons are detected, you are not to worry, but go through deliverance, and you will see a breakthrough in this area. I have seen many people been delivered from a spirit of madness and usually the cause of this was witchcraft being done to them.

Unforgiving Spirit

The demon of unforgiveness in another huge area that many people suffer from and usually the following spirits are associated with unforgiveness: Bitterness, Resentment, Anger, Stubbornness, Hard-heartedness and so forth. Remember what the Bible says: if we cannot forgive others, how will God forgive us from our sins? Many times I have noticed that people with grudges are not able to receive from the Holy Spirit due to a grudge they have been harbouring. Also, there will not be any deliverance taking place if you harbour unforgiveness towards someone. Take a pen now and test yourself, writing down all the people that have hurt you in the ast. Are you able to say their names out loud without feeling bitter or anger towards them? When you see them are you able to speak to them or hug them? If not, then there is a grudge you are harbouring or unforgiveness is in your against that person. Take this to the Lord daily and ask Him to help you forgive this person. Test yourself by buying a gift for them. Will you buy an honourable gift or something cheap that you know won't mean much to them?

Spirit Of Illness And Infirmity

This group of spirits is associated with illness and infirmity and I would group them in the following categories: Deaf spirit, spirit of infirmity (any kind of disease or illness), Death, Anorexia, Bulimia, Insomnia, Epilepsy, and so forth. There have been many times, while we are delivering people, that we have discerned the spirit of death. This could have entered into the person through praying to the dead, astral projecting, or through thoughts of suicide o witchcraft being done on that person. This needs immediate attention when going through deliverance.

Spirit Of Addiction

The next group of spirits would be anything a person can be addicted to, such as Alcohol, Nicotine, Cocaine, Heroin, Marijuana and nonprescription drugs, *etc*. Many times when I have started delivering someone, it is the spirit of addiction that I have found the easiest to deal with. Christians have been delivered from smoking, alcohol and even drugs. You may say, well, a person that is a Christian can't be addicted to drugs... well, actually, many times a person becomes a

Christian and they still have the spirit of addiction there and, unless they go through deliverance, this spirit will ultimately tempt them back into taking drugs, smoking or drinking, and may ultimately destroy their salvation.

False Religious And Idol-Worshipping Spirit

The next group of spirits would be the false religious spirits (Religious Spirit) or idolworshipping spirits (spiritual adultery spirit) and, once you practice one of these religions, through their initiations or incantations or 'special blessings and prayers', it is difficult to come out of these religions and many times people need to be delivered from the spirits behind these religions. Many of these religions will even have people worshipping idols or images, which are all entry points for demons to enter your life.

Poverty Spirit

The final groups of spirits that many people suffer from is the spirit of Poverty and the following demons are associated with these and they are: greed, stinginess, poverty, lack, debt, devouring spirit, spirit of failure, laziness and unproductivity.

Every one of these spirits brings a particular situation or a bigger, stronger demon in: for instance, if a person has a spirit of greed or stinginess, then it is very unlikely for that person to prosper because, again, it goes against the word of Jesus in Luke 6: 38 (*"Give and it will be given to you, good, measured, pressed down, shaken together, shall men be giving unto you."*) Hence, when people don't give to the needy, or to God's work, then they are operating under a spirit of greed and those people – according to the words of Jesus Christ of Nazareth

– will not prosper as people will not give to them. Hence, do you see how a spirit can bring problems in your life (*ie.* financial problems) if you do not cultivate a spirit of giving?

I have seen, so many times, the devouring spirit that takes everything from a believer due to the person unwilling to give tithes and offerings into the spiritual storehouse (the church). God warns in Malachi 3: 16 that, if we do not give our tithes and offerings, then a devouring spirit will devour our finances. Many people in the church today have this spirit operating in their lives and it is sad to see how they suffer financially. Some even give tithes, but do not give offerings generously, and again they do not prosper due to their lack of giving. They are willing to give to their friends and family generously but not to the work of God, the Bible says to give God the best of your offerings. There is a reason for everything the Bible says, yet we are so stubborn in following the word of God precisely, hence the many problems Christians face.

Some people even get financial miracles: God has extended their financial territory to double and even triple what came before. You may notice how everything improves in their life, but not their giving into the Kingdom of God, and yet they expect the Lord to move more in their finances; how can He when they are not trustworthy with the increase given unto them! Command the spirit of greed to leave when you are commanding the spirit of poverty and lack to, (these work hand-in-hand) and see what happens when you open your hand in giving to God's work!

Chapter 6
Spirits and their functions explained in more detail

I will spend some time in this chapter discussing certain types of spirits in more depth, their functions and how to recognise them.

Jezebel Spirit

This is a very evil spirit and you can read about this spirit in 1 Kings. Jezebel (a false prophetess who worshipped Baal) was married to King Ahab and controlled the King and all of Israel. The person who operates in this spirit will always make out they are 'holy' and usually operate with prophecies, which are false. They will, at the beginning, show they are submissive, but they are not, and inwardly rebelling against the church's authority, especially against the true prophets.

The person with this demon will work their way to the top, befriending the leadership and trying to help in all areas of the church and gain authority – eg. as a leader or even a minister! They will usually try to have their family members and close friends involved in all areas of the church so they can control what is being said and done in each area of the ministry.

This person will always hate true men and women of God, especially the true prophets. Look at how Jezebel tried to kill Elijah in 1 Kings 19. Once they are at the top, usually as the leader's 'right hand', they will start controlling and manipulating the leader, and trying to copy their style in releasing the anointing, but nothing will happen.

Once they get to the top, the leader comes under the Spirit of Jezebel and, instead of obeying the voice of the Holy Spirit, they are obeying the voice of Jezebel, a demon spirit! This will ultimately destroy the leadership, the anointing and the church! If the man or woman of God knows which demon is in operation, opposes this spirit and do not give it authority, then the person operating under Jezebel will start speaking against them to other members. If members are not careful they, too, will come under the spirit of Jezebel and rebel against the leadership and finally leave the church they are supposed to be in. This person (or persons) will be under the spirit of Ahab; they fear Jezebel and do all that she says. Jezebel will use Ahab, manipulating them in doing all that they say and even financially or materially use their resources.

It is very sad to see the spirit of Jezebel operating and, if you feel you have this spirit, you need to immediately confess your sin and seek a true and powerful deliverance ministry to help you come out of this spirit's hold.

Leviathan spirit

The Leviathan spirit is an extremely proud spirit and the Bible talks about this spirit in Isaiah 27:1 and Job 42. I would say next to Jezebel, this is just as bad and many people suffer from this spirit. The spirit of Leviathan can retaliate in the following ways if it feels it has been undermined in any shape or form:

1. The spirit in the person will retaliate very harshly if confronted
2. It can become violent and very angry through the person who has Leviathan

3. It will seek out revenge on anyone who undermines its power or authority
4. It will seek to destroy the person that has undermined it
5. It will never admit it's wrong or its defeat
6. It will always have an attitude of knowing it all or always being right in everything it says or does
7. It is very deceiving and twists the truth believing that everything the person who has this spirit says is truth, which is not
8. The person who operates under Leviathan cannot be tamed
9. It will make people leave churches and will always undermine the leadership and the authority of the church, thus causing division
10. Its words are destructive and have a negative effect on people
11. It is always critical of others and judgemental and especially those that are in authority. Thus making the person who has the spirit have a harsh heart
12. It will also mock others

The Bible says that God opposes the proud. When a man or woman suffer with this spirit, they are quarrelsome and there is always strife wherever they go as they feel the need to be recognised. God cannot use a man or woman with this spirit and the person suffering with this spirit will ultimately fall from any position of authority given to them by God. Instead of being remorseful and repentant, he or she will have a *'How dare they?'* attitude and will seek to avenge itself.

I have seen great people of God that are anointed vessels but due to Leviathan entering and operating they have fallen from their positions within church. It is very sad to see that they never realised they were under an extremely proud spirit and everything they try to do in life, God will oppose them.

Look at what happened to satan, he fell from heaven due to becoming very proud and formed a rebellion against God with thousands of other demons. This was all due to one emotion operating – pride. So be very careful that a door isn't opened to this spirit and if it is, seek that the Lord shuts it very quickly and that you are set free from the Spirit of Leviathan.

Ahab Spirit

The spirit of Ahab is usually the husband or the friend of the woman who has the Jezebel Spirit. This spirit is just like Ahab in the Bible, who was completely under the control of Jezebel, and even fears the woman that has the Jezebel spirit. Without them knowing, they become her helper and/or assistant in destroying the man or woman of God or church by spreading rumours, getting people on their side, and operating under deception by speaking false prophesies. Once a person is under the spirit of Jezebel as an Ahab, it is very difficult for him or her to see through it. Usually, they are completely deceived, thinking that whatever the person who operates under Jezebel says is right. There is also a big element of fear; they are continuously controlled and too scared to stand up to Jezebel.

Women who move with Jezebel will try to seduce men, too, and flirt with them to gain more power and control over them. In church, people (men or women) who have Ahab will not participate in anything unless the spirit of Jezebel in the person agrees to it and, even in that, they are controlled as to what to say and do. It's as if they are not allowed to think for themselves when they are under the spirit of Jezebel. I have seen this spirit operate on a number of occasions, and it is devastating in how they control people and the destruction they bring to their lives (and even the church) if the church does not oppose this demon spirit. I call it *'Stung by Jezebel'*. A church cannot even grow when such a spirit is operating through a person that likes to have control over all areas of the church, participates in everything and always has a say on every matter. You will even notice that all the problems in the church come from Jezebel and are supported by the Ahab that is following her. People don't even want to serve in church when the woman with Jezebel is operating in a place of God, as they feel intimidated and worried about what she will think or do. The spirit of fear comes upon them and the person with the Ahab spirit will particularly come under fear due to already being under the spirit of Jezebel. A person who has this spirit will always be a thorn in the church's side! A church will not be able to grow or move forward because there is a Jezebel spirit operating in the church.

Control And Manipulation

The spirit of control and manipulation is a very dominant spirit that will always try to be in control of every situation or circumstance. This spirit will try to control others and, if they cannot control them, it will aim to get its way through manipulating people into doing what it wants. This spirit will never want to be at the bottom but, like Jezebel, will always aim to be at the top and ahead in every situation. Once this spirit controls a person, they will usually use fear, manipulation and intimidation to control another person. It is a very dangerous spirit to come under and, once the person comes under this spirit, they will not be able to do anything or move freely unless the person agrees or tells them when they can do something. There is no free will and no freedom in a relationship when this spirit is in control. The spirit will demand and command you to do as they say and, if it is not done, that is when fear and intimidation comes in. Many times the spirits of anger and violence are also connected when a person is operating under control and manipulation.

Spirit Of Addiction

The spirit of addiction can be anything a person is addicted to, *ie.* smoking, alcohol, cannabis, heroin, addiction, *etc.* Many Christians, even after they become born again, are still addicted to certain substances. The most usual substance I have seen Christians addicted to for many years is nicotine. Many of these Christians have tried everything to stop smoking such as attending special 'Stop Smoking Clinics', using cigarette patches, *etc.* However, none of these have actually worked for the Christian due to the power of the spirit of addiction over the person's life. However, after one deliverance session, the spirit has left their lives and, after a long time of smoking, they do not feel the need or urge to pick up a cigarette again and that is through the power of deliverance! Isn't it awesome? By doing self-deliverance or attending a one-on-one or group deliverance session, you can be set free from smoking!

Spirit Of Lust And Seduction

A huge topic is the spirit of lust: many people I have come across have this spirit. Lust is mostly sexual: that is, lusting after people sexually. However, lust could also be lusting after material artefacts such as a car or a house. Lust can actually drive the person to commit all sorts of evil, especially when it comes to sexual acts. Many times you notice certain people, even in a good place, suddenly fall into extra-marital affairs, and you sit wondering how on Earth this could happen. One minute they are preaching the gospel, evangelising to the nations of the Earth, and the next they are having a scandalous affair. There goes their ministry, their credibility, the respect and honour of people they previously held. Why? Because of a demon called lust! Yes, it is very powerful, and one can be overcome by it if that person does not know, understand or undergo deliverance. Even if they do, by not examining themselves daily or being careful of the way they live (as many do), sins are more likely to become part of their life. This will all open doors to the demons of lust to take control, and the person will fall. It is always very sad to see this happen, even with great people of God that we so admire and respect. But demons do not respect your position within a church; if there is an open door, then they are in it to kill, steal and destroy! Christians wake up to this; this is real and, there is no point blaming everyone else and their circumstance. What you need to understand is that the fight against the dark world is real, as the Bible says that we do not battle against flesh and blood but against the principalities of the dark world. When are we going to get it? When? If you feel you have this spirit, do not be ashamed, but approach a spiritual person who deals with deliverance and be willing to undergo the process. As long as you live right, you will not regret it, but be thankful you were willing to set your pride aside and go through deliverance. And, yes, there will be a battle, no-one says it is easy, but as long as you are willing, God will be willing through His precious Holy Spirit and the name above all names, Jesus Christ of Nazareth, to deliver you with His awesome power!

There is also the Spirit of Seduction, which is used mainly by women to seduce men. Many times in the church you see men strong in the faith fall, and usually there is a spirit of lust operating through the man and the spirit of seduction operating through the woman. A woman who moves in seduction will wear revealing outfits in church; she will dance in a seducing manner, smile, and talk seductively. Many times you will notice this woman will be trying to seduce men of God with her mannerisms, and many times people don't understand the spirit she is operating under – it actually becomes shameful and embarrassing to watch! Many times, even the woman doesn't realise that she is operating under this spirit, and it is actually seducing men to fall into temptation and, ultimately, sin. That is why the Bible warns us, in 1 Timothy 2: 9–10, that women should dress respectably with modesty and apparel, and also for people not to be a stumbling block to others (1 Corinthians 8:9). Hence, if you feel that you are flirtatious, then ask yourself what spirit you are operating under and ask the Lord to deliver you. Don't allow people to point fingers at you that you seduce men of God with your behaviour. Men can also have this spirit and they, too, should examine themselves if they have a seducing spirit.

Deception

Many people move under the spirit of deception. They think it is God telling them something to say or do, but actually there is another demon operating. Many times they even think the Lord showed them something, but it is not the case; they are moving under deception. How sad to see this spirit operating in the church and with so many Christians. I have noticed this particularly with people who have not been through deliverance, and they think that everything they hear is from God, where it actually is from a spirit of deception. That is why the Bible says to test every spirit (in 1 John 4: 11) because there is so much deception in the church and amongst believers. If you think you are under the spirit of deception, then immediately start with self-deliverance and check it out, when you command it to leave your life, is anything going. Ask and pray to the Lord about it: you don't want this demon to be operating in your life.

Religious Spirit

Many people operate under this spirit, which we call the Spirit of Religiosity. This spirit is very deceptive; people with this spirit always come across as highly spiritual and God-fearing, but yet they do not have a deep relationship with the Lord; it is all on the surface. Moreover, people with this spirit never move in freedom and always are religious with everything. They never allow the Spirit of the Lord to move freely in a meeting, they always try to limit the anointing as they may feel this is not of God, and they always feel that certain things have to be done in a certain way and in a certain time. For example, they will always look at a time for everything and prefer to stick to time rather than allow the Holy Spirit to have his way in the service. People that don't do it their way and are free in Christ within church are usually looked down upon by people with the religious spirit. When someone operates in this spirit, they preach strict law, and never the freedom that Christ offers. They also look down upon people they consider unworthy or the way these people praise God. Do not be deceived: a person who operates like this is operating under Religiosity, and not in the freedom that Christ gives us.

Rebellious Spirit

This spirit is evident in many people I have ministered and pastored, and it is the spirit of rebelliousness. This spirit does not accept any authority over the person they inhabit, whether this authority comes from parents, church, work, or even the Government. Many people have this spirit and, because of the rebellious spirit, will not be able to use that person fully, as the person who operates under this spirit does not accept any command from the Lord or any spiritual or physical authority. The person who has this spirit will always think they know better, even if they are not experienced enough: they will not sit at the feet of people of God to be mentored; they will not adhere to any policies or protocol of the church or work. When the Lord or a man or woman of God gives them guidance, they are not willing to take it on board, and rebel against all that the church or any authority may say. With some people, this spirit is very evident, and it will always come against the leaders and the authority of the church. A person who operates under the spirit of rebelliousness will not go very far in the ways of God, as the Lord cannot trust them with the anointing or the work he has for that person. Satan has managed to use this spirit incredibly against children of God, as this holds many blessings and promotions from the person. The person will then start blaming God that their lives are not moving forward, but they do not realise that they have given Satan a legal right to hold their blessings and promotions due to the spirit of rebelliousness.

The reason people have this spirit is because at some point in their lives, usually in their childhood or teens, they may have been under a controlling person, such as a father who would not allow them to go out and have fun. Anger, resentment and disappointment will enter this person, and will give the right for rebelliousness to enter. You may hear women saying, "I will never allow any man to boss me around". The reason is because this woman was, at some point, controlled by a man in her life, and hence it has opened a door to a spirit of rebelliousness. The person does not realise this demon will have a significant effect on their later lives, both spiritually and physically. Check yourself: when someone tells you to do something, how do you react? Many times you may say 'okay' to the request, but within you, there are bad thoughts coming into your mind about that person, which is a spirit of rebelliousness. Pray to the Lord to deliver you from this spirit and ask God to give you a teachable and willing spirit.

I remember once I asked God how obedient He wants us to be and He showed me a vision of His angels. He showed me that, before the word even leaves the Lord's mouth, the angels have already gone off to perform what God is asking of them. The Lord showed me that that is how obedient He wants us to be. Awesome!

Medium Spirit

The medium spirit is a spirit of divination: a false prophecy demon. This spirit operates through people who many times tell you about your past but for no particular reason, *ie.* to confess your sins, which will bring about deliverance. Many people start believing what they say about the church and others is the truth, but it actually is deception. The reason people believe them is because they were right about their past and, hence, they must be right about another Christian or the church. These are completely false as they are operating under a spirit of divination. This spirit must not be allowed to operate in the church as many will fall into deception if it is allowed to continue.

Witchcraft

Witchcraft is a very evil spirit to be operating in a person. The spirit comes upon a man or woman and, through the power of this spirit, the person starts to cast spells or uses witchcraft to do different things to people, whether Christians or non-Christians. Many born-again believers think they cannot be bewitched, but look at what Apostle Paul says to the Galatians in Galatians 3:1: *"Who has bewitched you?"*. Also, in the New Testament, one reads about Simon the Sorcerer, who wanted to buy the disciples' power to use, as it was more powerful than his own evil power. So, do not be deceived, this spirit is real, and is operating in churches through people who claim to be Christians, but are using the power of witchcraft to do evil to people. As a Pastor and Deliverance Minister, I have spent many hours casting this spirit out of people that have been bewitched through witchcraft. Once, I asked the Lord why would people do this to others, and the Lord showed me they were initiated. For example, there are some temptations you may not be able to get out of doing; it is the same for these people that operate in this power. We do not hate them but the sin they are involved in.

Spiritual Husbands/ Wives

This is a topic that is hardly ever discussed in churches, and if it is, it's a hush-hush topic. Many people haven't even heard of the term 'spiritual husband' or 'spiritual wife'. However, this is a very real topic, and something that needs to be addressed. Many women or men, due to sexual sins in the past, have opened themselves up to a spiritual wife or husband. These demons will actually come at night and have sex with the person in their dreams. Sometimes the person may see someone they know (or do not know) having sex with them in the dream, and other times the person may actually feel something or someone having real sexual relations with them at night. I have known of many cases being involved in deliverance of people suffering with this spirit.

Many times they think it is normal, but it is not; God wants us to be pure, and how can you be when there is a demon having sexual relations with you at night? Sometimes people have been initiated and 'married' to demon spirits when they were much younger (particularly in certain cultures) and this spirit actually becomes their husband or wife. You may be suffering with this every night, once a week or once a month. Sometimes a woman may be having 'sex in the dream' when they are about to come onto their menstrual cycle. This is not normal – don't be deceived. There is a spiritual husband or wife that has been sent to afflict you.

If you are experiencing this, you need to go through deliverance. You will probably think it is normal or you may feel guilty or ashamed. You don't need to feel this way, but repent of any doors you have opened in the spirit through sexual sins or watching pornography, *etc*. You need to find a deliverance ministry that understand and deals with these issues and ask to go through deliverance, and every night, you need to ask the Lord to consecrate you and command no demon to touch you in Jesus' name, as you belong to God. Do not suffer with this anymore, but be set free with the power and the name of Jesus. It is only Jesus that can heal and set you free from demons plaguing your life. Take control now and do not put up with this any more.

Spirit Of Torment

Spirit of torment is a spirit that is always tormenting people through the mind. It usually brings bad thoughts to the person, such as low self-esteem, guilt, self-hate, rejection, and extreme fear about every situation and everyone. People with this spirit find it very challenging to serve God and be in church, they constantly feel tormented, and have no peace within them. Usually, you will see them being like a yo-yo, one day they are okay and the next day down, because of a spirit tormenting their life. They may think that everyone does not like them or accepts them in a place (this is the spirit of rejection). You see, one spirit can be associated with many other spirits, and all are focused on ruining Christians and bringing destruction to your life.

Chapter 7
Becoming a Deliverance Minister

If people want to cast demons out of others, I believe they need to be in the right place to receive the training and anointing to cast devils out. I have known people trying to cast out a spirit for hours with nothing happening. I will ask the question, "How can you cast out devils when you have many spirits in you?". There is no authority there, because you have never taken the authority to cast out your own spirits; how can you do deliverance on others? You may say that they have bigger spirits – how do you know if you haven't been through the process yourself? You may say that you do not have the drinking problem that the person you are trying to cast demons out of has… yes, but you may have the spirit of Jezebel, which is even more problematic!

In order to operate in deliverance, you need to go through it yourself; you need to be anointed and given the authority by the Holy Spirit and by the church's authority to cast demons out of people. God respects the church's authority, and the anointing flows downwards when there is respect and honour of the authority God has placed above you. The Bible says in 1 Corinthians 14: 33 that God is a God of order, and He will not do the opposite of the authority placed over the church.

Also, you need to have been anointed for this ministry, you may want to be a deliverer, you may have been discipled by men and women of God to do the ministry of Jesus, and that is to cast spirits out. However, you need to have been given the authority and the anointing to do so. Remember in Acts 19: 11–20, when the sons of Skiva tried to cast demons out of the one man; what did the demons in the man do? They hit them, saying, "Jesus we know, Paul we know, but who are you?" This shows that spirits will only respect the anointing and the authority given to people of God for this ministry. Deliverance is a serious matter; please do not take it lightly. The other problem that can happen in deliverance is that your spirits can be transferred onto the person who is trying to deliver you, and vice versa. Again, I have seen this happen, and therefore as ministers and pastors we need to be under the leadership of the Holy Spirit as to who we allow in our ministries to lay hands on people to either pray or cast spirits out.

Chapter 8
My personal experience of deliverance

I was in a lovely church that did not move in the anointing, the power of God, healing or deliverance. They were nice people; however, I wanted and needed more, and felt that everything in my life was stagnant. I felt nothing was moving and I was so hungry for more of God's presence and glory upon my life. I needed more of Him, I needed more of His presence upon my life, yet I felt things were not right in me. I was not living in sin, tried to live a righteous life, gave my tithes and offerings, worked hard, attended church and served every Sunday without complaining. I spent time every morning and early evening praying, fellowshipped with Christians who took their walk with God seriously, read the Word of God and watched Christian TV. That was my life as a young person in my early twenties, yet something wasn't right, and I knew it! I could not put my finger on it, something big was out of place and, yes, I was born again and baptised in the Holy Spirit; yet I could not understand the inner conflicts I had, and nothing made me happy or content, no matter what I achieved or did.

One day I met a man of God and he was shining, to the point that I found myself staring at him, because he was just shining so much. I kept on asking myself what it was: why was this man shining? What did he have? There must be something I am missing! What made it worse was that I had met this man two years prior, and he was completely different, to the point that I had warned a sister in the Lord to stay away from him due to the way he behaved, and now I said to the same woman that this man is different, he has changed, what could it be…?.I wanted to know what was upon this man: what had made him look so different to the man he was. When I had met him before, there was no peace, and no calmness about him. However, now he was the complete opposite, full of tranquillity and serenity.

Finally, the man started talking to us about deliverance (with caution, as he knew we were conservative in our thinking and very traditional). When he said to me that I could have spirits inhabiting my life, I laughed and said, "no way, that can't be true!" and brushed it aside… he then gave me a book to read on deliverance and I took it with me on holiday. I prayed before reading the book, asking the Lord that, if this is true, to show me and deliver me. Instantly, deliverance started in my life, and I knew without a shadow of a doubt that this was true and Christians need deliverance! Yes, even Christians like me, who had never done – in my mind – any 'major' sins. I was focused on serving the Lord, but yet I, too, needed to be spiritually cleaned up, and that is what deliverance does! Do not be afraid of deliverance, have an open heart and spirit and see what God will do! In five years' time, you will look back and won't believe you are the same person, all because you have allowed God to do a supernatural work in you! Awesome! Thank you, Jesus, for deliverance and what you are teaching your people!

I could not wait to get back home to the UK and talk to this man more about my experience with self-deliverance. Upon my return, he explained that there were group deliverance sessions at his church, and I immediately agreed to go to these. I wanted to be delivered; I wanted a change in my spiritual and physical life; I needed more of the Holy Spirit; I just needed more! I was so excited about it and was willing to go all the way with deliverance no matter what!

That was where it all started for me: the whole new world of being set free as a born-again Christian.

 Many times we do not have a clue about what spirits inhabit our lives, but if only we are willing to go through this, it will change our lives for the better. I saw so many things that had left my own life, and yet, I had not done half the things others had done, as I grew up in a conservative family. But there were spirits in my life. So when people say that deliverance is only for the drug addicts or the alcoholics, it is not, because here I was, stayed away from unrighteous living from an early age, and yet spirits where inhabiting my very own life. I believe that everyone needs to go through deliverance, but not everyone is ready for deliverance, due to the fact of the lifestyle they are living. The more deliverance you go through, the more the power, the anointing and the Holy Spirit can inhabit your life, and the more God can use you for His glory. People will look at you and even say you are different, you are peaceful, and you have a beautiful spirit, because of being cleaned up.

 Usually, people that have been through deliverance and maintain their deliverance shine with God's presence: they look younger and they are more powerful in their prayers. You can see the difference with people who have been through true deliverance. The reason I say 'true' is because some people say they have been through deliverance, but it is not the deliverance preached about (such as these spirits actually coming out by the person coughing out or vomiting out or shrieking out or feeling that something has left). They command spirits to leave, but they actually don't leave. So, although some may say it's deliverance, it is not, as it's not the way Jesus did it. When Jesus commanded spirits to leave a person's life, they would come out vomiting, foaming at the mouth, coughing, screaming, and spitting: that is evidence that deliverance is actually taking place. However, be warned, as many times a spirit can actually be putting on a show. They may be coughing or screaming, but not actually coming out, due to a hold or a door or a legal right in that person's life, such as an unconfessed sin. Many times, as I have been delivering people, the demon is actually manifesting, but not coming out, and when I enquire from the Holy Spirit what is happening, the Lord shows me that, due to the person not confessing their sin in this area, the demon still has a legal right to inhabit the person's life. Hence, I immediately ask the person to confess their sin in their mind and repent and then, almost immediately, deliverance starts taking place!

This may be a new area for you; you may have been like me, not knowing that demons exist, and they can even oppress your life. But be open to deliverance, as many of the problems you are facing are actually a spiritual problem, and you need to go through deliverance to overcome these. Do not be frightened, but embrace this new-found knowledge, and ask the Lord to lead you to a good deliverance ministry where you can be set free and experience all that God has for your life. It is time to command spirits plaguing your life, your family, your marriage, your finances, your emotions, your mind, and your business to leave in Jesus' name. It worked for me, and so many others I have ministered to, through the power of the Holy Spirit, and it will work for you. But ensure you live right, be in a place where the anointing and presence of God moves, and see that you will be victorious in all areas of your life. When I went through deliverance, I felt so much freedom and the glory of the Lord was upon my life, and He was able to use me powerfully for His work. I thank the Lord that He taught me about this very special area, and I pray and believe your time has now come to experience victorious living through the power of deliverance!

Chapter 9
Test your knowledge on deliverance

1. Where in the Bible does it say to cast demons out?
2. What is the difference between oppression and possession?
3. How does a person behave when they are possessed?
4. What do we mean by rightful covering and anointing?
5. Why is it important to live right?
6. What did Jesus warn us about when spirits left our lives?
7. Can you name the different areas a spirit can gain access in your life?
8. What do we mean by putting the wooden doors?
9. In Biblical terms what do we mean when we talk about the spirit of Jezebel?
10. If you wanted to be a deliverance minister, what would you need to do?

Personal notes you would like to make on reading this book

Maria Yiangou

Dear Reader,

We would love for you to share what God has been doing to your life now that you know about deliverance and write to us by becoming a monthly partner. Your partnership will help us and our ministry spread the Good News, the message of salvation, breakthrough, healing, prosperity and deliverance for believers across the world through our television broadcasts, webcasts and conferences.

Please do write to us,

God Bless,

Pastors Andy & Maria
Victory in Christ Ministries, London, England

Receive all these benefits by becoming a partner with the Ministry of Pastor Andy & Maria Yiangou:

- Bi-monthly letters
- Special Offers
- Announcements of new books by Pastors Andy & Maria
- Invitation to special events, conferences and
- seminars
- Access to our Prayer Hopeline
- Free products available to partners i.e. CDs and DVDs

Deliverance – Your Key to Freedom

Dear Pastor Andy & Maria,

Please place these prayer requests on the Miracle Prayer Altar at Victory in Christ Ministries in London, England to be prayed for:

1. _____

2. _____

3. _____

4. _____

5. _____

Enclosed is my love gift of £/$/€ _____ to help you win souls and spread the healing, breakthrough and deliverance message.

Yes, I want to be a monthly partner to help you reach the nations of the world and receive even more anointed teaching. Enclosed is my first months commitment of £/$/€_____. Please start writing to me and send me my membership benefits.

Name _____

Surname _____

Address _____

City _____

State/Province _____

Postal Code --

Country --

Phone Number --

E- mail --

Post today to Pastors Andy & Maria Yiangou. Please log onto the website for details of the address www.victoryinchrist.co.uk or call 0044 203 151 3798

Invite the Pastors to one of your speaking engagements by contacting Victory in Christ Ministries.

Deliverance – Your Key to Freedom

www.ingramcontent.com/pod-product-compliance
Lightning Source LLC
Chambersburg PA
CBHW021136300426
44113CB00006B/447